Coping with Depression

'Depression is as universal as the common cold. It can be so slight as to be hardly worth the name – just a passing mood which will be gone tomorrow. It can be a vague feeling of persistent dreariness that takes the sparkle out of life as we carry on with the usual routine. Or, at the other extreme, it can almost totally paralyse action . . .'

What causes depression? How can we recognize it, in ourselves and in others? And what help is available? Myra Chave-Jones is a practising psychotherapist and a Christian. She writes with a deep understanding and sympathy for those living under the dark shadow of depression – isolated and helpless – for whom it seems 'always winter and never Christmas'. Her book is full of clear information and practical examples.

She writes not only for those suffering depression, but also for all who live close to them. She describes what depression feels like, the treatments, those who may be specially at risk. She deals with the factors of guilt and religious doubt. She also offers constructive help in handling depression and in avoiding its recurrence.

COPING WITH DEPRESSION

Myra Chave-Jones

A LION PAPERBACK

Copyright © 1981 Myra Chave-Jones

Published by
Lion Publishing plc
Icknield Way, Tring, Herts, England
ISBN 0 85648 360 5
Lion Publishing Corporation
1705 Hubbard Avenue, Batavia, Illinois 60510, USA
ISBN 0 85648 360 5
Albatross Books Pty Ltd
PO Box 320, Sutherland, NSW 2232, Australia
ISBN 0 86760 282 1

First edition 1981
Reprinted 1982, 1983, 1984, 1985 (twice), 1986

All names and examples used in this book
are fictitious

Printed in Great Britain by
Richard Clay (The Chaucer Press) Ltd,
Bungay, Suffolk

Contents

To Pearl
– who stood by me unswervingly
when I was depressed

Introduction

Depression is as universal as the common cold. It can be so slight as to be hardly worth the name – just a passing mood which will be gone tomorrow. It can be a vague feeling of persistent dreariness which takes the sparkle out of life as we carry on with the usual routine. Or, at the other extreme, it can almost totally paralyse action, making us unable to carry out the simplest tasks, and even to lose interest in life itself.

Depression may last for only a short time, or it may drag on for months, even years. It is the sort of sunless, snowclad climate which the children in the Narnia stories of C. S. Lewis describe as 'always winter and never Christmas'.

Like the common cold, in its persistent form it is a type of ill health and needs to be recognized as such. Unfortunately, physical illness seems often to be more socially acceptable than an emotional illness like depression. Onlookers are usually much more sympathetic to a physically identifiable illness which can be seen or understood. But depression is a very painful emotional condition. It can at times make life very burdensome for the sufferer, and very trying for those around him.

People suffering from depression feel isolated, helpless and unlovable. The dreariness and heaviness they feel quickly communicates itself to other people, so that they tend to withdraw. Even reading about depression can be a dreary business! It seems as though the depressed person is inside a dense fog. Although he is calling for help he feels that no one can see and reach him. The people on the outside may be trying their level best to make contact but there seems to be an invisible wall preventing them from getting in touch.

It may be this sense of mutual frustration which makes depression such an 'infectious' condition. It is quite possible for the prevailing spirit of the whole community to be depressed, quite apart from the reactions of individual people within it. The general sense of futility, the possibility of another war, the loss of national identity, the depersonalization brought about by high technology, are some of the reasons for the underlying depression in many Western countries today. This depression in turn contributes to the malaise, violence and general unhappiness which exists in the community. So it is vitally important that we understand and learn to cope with depression, for the sake of the individual and of society as a whole.

Some people blame the decline in religion. Not the sort of hypocritical piety which can co-exist with injustice, dishonesty and sordidness – we could do with a decline in that! But the loss of wholehearted, confident Christian faith which gives purpose to living and shows the way to a new quality of life – loving, forgiving, and caring.

Depression is often linked with some problem in trusting. Before we can trust, we need to know that the person concerned is to be trusted. The Christian faith introduces men and women to a God who can always be trusted, whose word is his bond and whose love is unchanging, strong, true, predictable, and concerned for their deepest good. It therefore has something to say about depression, and something vital to offer those who are in the depths.

Chapter One

Physical Causes

Every one of us – every individual person – is unique. No one else has precisely the same combination of factors which add up to make one particular human being. Even within the same family no two people inherit exactly the same genes. Neither have they had precisely the same emotional and social experiences in life. Although an observer may sometimes find it hard to detect differences, there are subtle variations (even in the case of identical twins).

Our heredity, our biochemistry, our early emotional and physical environment and our experiences in adult life all influence the way we react to stress at any given time. So it is essential to look at our whole selves – our mind, our body, the inner world of our emotions and fantasies, the outer world of our experiences and relationships – in trying to understand the causes of depression.

Healthy reaction
Depression is sometimes a healthy reaction to stress, following a sustained period of intense mental or physical exertion. This is often the reason for the flatness, the feeling of pointlessness which follows the output of concentrated energy.

'Post Wimbledon blues' could be a feature for tennis players. The aftermath of important exams is often, 'I've made a hopeless mess. I don't care anyway. The whole thing isn't worth while.' Or months of caring for an aged relative can produce an overwhelming sense of not being able to carry on.

Nature has a marvellous inbuilt compensatory system, sending signals about the need for rest and recovery which will restore our balance automatically.

Heredity deals the cards

One of the things over which the individual has no control is the 'pack of cards' each of us inherits at birth. We have been given the colour of our eyes and hair, the shape of our features, and temperamental predispositions. Some of us have a flying start; others have a fairly unremarkable list of assets! We have to play these 'cards' as best we can in the game of life. As in a game of Monopoly, we also have to encounter life's 'chances' and 'community chests'. There is no opting out of the joys and sorrows that come our way. We can't stop the world and get off!

Because life is unpredictable and opportunities are so unequal, many people today go along with the existentialist view that life has no meaning and we must therefore live for the passing moment. Reporting the death of Jean-Paul Sartre, one of the leading proponents of existentialism, a news announcer came out with this astonishing statement: '. . . Jean-Paul Sartre believed that life had no meaning, so we should live it up ... He has given hundreds of people a new meaning to life'!

In reality this defeatist and despairing attitude brings a different and very negative perspective, but hardly a new meaning, to life. The increasing interest in meditation and mysticism is in itself evidence of our inborn conviction that there is more to life than we can see, even if we cannot understand it. The Christian's perception of a God who has something to say to a despairing world is shot through with encouragement and solid hope.

The Bible says that in spite of the inequalities and adversities of life there is a God whose nature is unchanging love, strength and wisdom. In every circumstance, if we will only turn to him, he is ready to guide and help. God has not promised equal opportunities to everyone. And human greed and inhumanity make very sure that inequality is a permanent feature of life. But God is just and true – something different from and more far reaching than being 'fair'. The Bible also says that God himself in the person of Jesus Christ has shared our human suffering in order to break its total power.

No other philosophy or religion can offer such a Saviour. Many sensible, thinking people have found these claims a reality in their experience. Their lives have been changed as a result of knowing God in a direct and personal way.

But, Christian or non-Christian, we still have to reckon with our human heredity. Some people have a predisposition towards a depressive personality. They can quote examples of other members of their family who have been beset at times by black moods. It may actually help to know this, if depression is one of the handicaps against which we struggle. It can then be recognized as an inbuilt difficulty, and this knowledge may reduce the sense of guilt, the 'I-ought-not-to-feel-like-this', that so often goes with depression.

It is only as we become more aware of our own make-up and personality – for good and ill – that we can set about modifying our behaviour so that other people, and we ourselves, find it more acceptable. And here the love, power and wisdom of God is available to help us.

Body chemistry out of balance

At times the proportions of various chemicals in our brain get out of balance. This seems to link with extremes of mood – and depression is commoner than elation. These mood changes are quite disproportionate to any actual difficulties or problems we may be faced with from the outside world.

This chemical imbalance may contribute to the depression that follows viral illnesses ('flu is a good example). It may accompany some major upheaval in our body hormones – the birth of a baby, or the menopause. Or there may be no known reason for this change in the body's chemistry. The experts still have a lot to learn about the relationship between the hidden working of the body's chemistry, which we cannot consciously control, and the effects it has on our moods and behaviour.

Jennifer Dean was a naturally happy, outgoing girl who had a depressive episode after the birth of her first baby, much to her own and everyone's surprise. Her marriage was good, the baby was planned and welcome and there seemed to be no reason for this reaction. Fortunately it lasted only a few weeks and she soon returned to her normal, cheerful self, under her doctor's care.

Chapter Two

Depression from Within

Every human being is by nature essentially a social being. We are inevitably influenced by our surroundings. We respond to the warmth and support of colleagues or to criticism and lack of appreciation from people at home. If we live in an emotionally cold environment where we do not seem to be cared for and supported, it is very easy for us to begin to feel undervalued and useless – a quick road to depression.

We have to cultivate our ability to stand on our own and not be too dependent on other people for our sense of wellbeing. It is easy to see how a growing baby learns to tolerate the absence of his mother for gradually increasing lengths of time. But there comes a point (at bedtime when he is tired, or when he hurts himself) when his reserves break down and he needs her comforting presence to reassure him.

As mature adults we are better able (hopefully) to maintain our own inner equilibrium in the face of difficulties. Nevertheless we do need loving relationships which encourage and give us a sense of confidence. As adults we are also able to form two-way relationships – unlike babies, who can think only of themselves and their own needs.

This may sound silly, but many people are affected by the weather. In Britain, February and March are often hard months to endure. Cold grey skies, day after day, produce (or reflect) an inner greyness of spirit.

Christmas, too, can bring its own kind of depression, especially if we are alone or sad. Everyone else's jollity (real or imagined) seems to highlight our own lack of happy relationships. The absence of family or friends becomes particularly conspicuous. This is especially acute when someone we love has died since the previous Christmas.

Childhood

The most formative factor in anyone's personality is the experience of the first five to seven years of life. The Jesuits discovered this long ago when they said: 'Give me a child until it is seven and I have it for the rest of its life.' In more recent times the importance of these early years to the adult has been researched and confirmed. The child is, in a real sense, 'father to the man'.

A tiny baby has no previous experience on which to build. Every stimulus and experience is making its first imprint. Who knows for sure what the baby may be thinking when he is safe in the womb? But his first conscious experience in the outside world must be really uncomfortable and traumatic – pushing and pulling, bright lights, loud noises, cold air, and a frightening nothingness engulfs him. This vulnerable and helpless creature is totally dependent on other people. They have to learn to be sensitive to his needs and understand the language of his movements and cries. His repertoire is very limited – though quite sufficient for most babies to communicate their basic needs!

He will soon begin to understand whether he is loved and welcomed. He will know if he is being nourished emotionally as well as physically, though he cannot distinguish between his inner and outer world. He responds to the security of firm, gentle hands and voice. He begins to feel safe and starts to trust. Feeding times (the main events of his day) will be a pleasurable and confirming experience. He will gradually absorb the love with which he is surrounded. At the same time he acquires a sense of being valued. He is too small to be articulate about it but he will know it clearly all the same.

This sense of trust and mutual response is the most important aspect of a healthy personality which parents can help their children to establish. *Everything* else is built on this foundation. As the child grows he will have his increasing trust reinforced many times a day by consistency in incidents too small to mention and big promises kept. Obviously, in every family, there will be times when his expectations are disappointed. But he will be able to tolerate minor frustrations, because basically he has no inner questions about whether he is loved. He will not need to adopt a repeated pattern of tantrums or manipulatory behaviour. He will be growing up in an atmosphere of loving trust and will breathe it like the air.

Any normal child will experiment to see how much his parents will tolerate, and will be disobedient or unco-operative from time to time.

This is how he learns about limits and about loving relationships. He may also have periods of doubt, as when a new baby arrives and he has less of his mother's attention than he used to. But he is relatively easy to reassure.

There is something irresistible about an alert, responsive baby with bright eyes and a ready smile. He seems to exude health and interest. And even when he is asleep his calm relaxation speaks for itself. His experience of life in his family is relatively unstressful.

Parents
But what about the parents? Some parents are by nature cold and distant. Some are tense, anxious and insecure. Some have been seriously deprived in some way. Some have been brought up by over-strict and critical, over-indulgent, or domineering parents. They do not have a good experience of firm, loving parents to pass on to their own children. This makes it difficult for them to give to their children a firm foundation of consistent, affirming love which is not afraid to stick to defined limits. This firm foundation is essential for emotional and also for physical health. Children are uncannily quick to pick up any weakness in their parents' attitudes and to reflect it in their own behaviour.

Brian's problem
Brian Fergusson is a highly competent man holding a responsible job. But his life is dogged by a constant sense of failure. At the end of each day he comes home exhausted and often irritable. He criticizes his own

standard of work. He feels that he gives inadequate support to the people who work with him. (In fact his work is of quite a high standard and his colleagues do find him supportive.)

He looks back over his early life, when he lived in constant fear of his strict and irascible father, who never seemed satisfied with Brian's efforts. When he produced a silver medal for sport, he was asked why it wasn't a gold. When he won a distinction in history, he was asked why he had not got one in English as well.

The fact that Brian is a sensitive, affectionate *person* seemed to escape notice. He was only valued by what he could achieve. Small wonder that he began to see himself in the same light, to believe that he was never good enough.

In addition to his actual experiences, Brian was reinforcing learned habit patterns, so that without realizing it he set things up to fail. It is a short step from that state of mind to depression.

David

David Martin was conceived 'accidentally' two weeks after his parents' wedding day. They were very much in love and had not planned to have a baby quite so soon. His mother was herself the eldest of several children and had had to be a little mother to them when she was young. She was therefore looking forward to basking in her husband's love and not having to share him with anybody. The news that she was pregnant was exceedingly unwelcome.

Even so, David's parents made all the preparations and were pleased with their little son when he arrived. But although they really loved him, there was also a great deal of hidden resentment on his mother's part at this hasty intrusion. She found it very difficult to be loving to him at times, when she was tired or distracted. He in turn became demanding or naughty, which set up a vicious circle.

I met David when he was three. I was struck by the wistful expression in his eyes and the fact that he was unduly compliant. Somehow he seemed to have picked up both the positive and also the very definitely negative attitudes of his mother towards him. In consequence he was confused and unsure of himself. The messages he is receiving in his early years will no doubt have some repercussions later on in life, unless they can be changed.

When a parent dies
The harsh events of the external world, too, can impinge on a child's life in a way which leaves lasting marks. His relationship with either parent may be broken by death, leaving him puzzled and sad. He has lost an important and irreplacable part of his life.

The adult concept of death is far beyond the understanding of his young mind. Like all children, he is only aware of experiences in relation to himself. So this unwelcome absence must somehow be because the departed person does not love him any more. He must be unlovable and bad. Somehow, in some way he does not know, he must have caused the person to go away.

This is a great mystery and a deep hurt. Although

small children are often fairly easily distracted, they will keep coming back to this unsolved mystery. Wise adult help is needed as they search their minds to know what they have done to cause this unpleasantness. Even if they are able to achieve some resolution, a big question-mark is often left. Are they really lovable, acceptable and good enough? There is documented evidence that a person bereaved in childhood is likely to be 'at risk' to depression in later life.

The broken home

These days it is rare for a child to be in a class at school where *all* his friends' parents are still living together. Death has always been a hazard, but now separation and divorce are a much greater threat to the trusting love of the child. Parental rows and absences are terribly frightening to him.

His whole safety still depends on his parents, so he is desperately threatened in a very fundamental way when he lies upstairs in the dark listening to the angry noises below, or when he sees his mother constantly fretful and anxious because once again Daddy is still not home. Again he relates all these in some cause-and-effect way to himself. A broken home frequently leaves a bruised child.

It is not only the break-up of their parents' relationship which is so very damaging for children. The separation caused by prolonged admission to hospital or to boarding school when the child is too emotionally tender to bear it can be very harmful.

Separation from someone we love is always

painful – to children and adults alike. It hits at our most vulnerable emotional areas. Adults can usually manage to contain the pain better than children, because of their more extensive life experience. But even so it *is* very painful.

Sarah

Sarah Ellison was four when her baby brother was born. She was sent to stay with a childless aunt, a stranger to her. And she had to stay there for two or three months after the birth because her mother was very ill. She didn't want to stay with the aunt and cried bitterly to go to her own home. She could not understand why people were stopping her seeing her Mummy. Neither could she understand that her aunt felt rejected by her endless misery. The child was ungrateful!

When Sarah's tears brought no resolution or relief she gradually cried less. But she also spoke and ate less and became increasingly apathetic. Very slowly she returned to normal life, but was quieter and more withdrawn. Externally life went on, and eventually she went home, but internally there was a deep wound.

Years later, when Sarah was training to be a physiotherapist, her great friend left the course to get married and go abroad. Sarah plummetted into a severe depression and had to be admitted to hospital for a while. With help, she began to feel and admit to all the deeply buried pain, fear and sense of guilt that separation from a loved person creates. It was a long, hard road to recovery.

The pain, doubt and questioning may never be

fully resolved for a child who has to experience prolonged separation at an age when he cannot be objective about it. He may appear to acclimatize, and observers may comment how well he has accepted it.

As human beings we cannot live in a perpetual state of intense pain. So, much of the feeling associated with a traumatic experience gets absorbed into the borders of consciousness, or is driven underground and carried along into adult life. We may develop a fundamentally pessimistic personality, finding it easy to believe the worst – although we may also have fun and enjoyment. Depression never feels far from the surface and any situation of stress can easily activate it.

The particular details of childhood experiences will have been forgotten long ago. But the internal atmosphere of consistent self-doubt, apprehension, timidity, or the ready feeling of being unloved, will persist. These feelings are sometimes masked by a blustering, bombastic and apparently conceited exterior.

Fortunately, however, there is usually an opportunity to repair the damage which may have been caused inadvertently in early years. We often find good friends, or a marriage partner, who will help us to build again the broken walls of trust and self-respect.

The case of Eeyore!

A.A. Milne captured individual personalities superbly in the delightful characters of Christopher Robin's friends – phlegmatic Pooh, bouncing Tigger, nervous Piglet and the rest. And Eeyore. To

Eeyore it seemed that everyone else always ate his food, went to parties without him, or left him out in the rain.

One day, 'Eeyore, the old grey donkey, stood by the side of the stream and looked at himself in the water. "Pathetic," he said, "that's what it is. Pathetic." He turned and walked slowly down the stream for twenty yards, splashed across it, and walked slowly back on the other side. Then he looked at himself in the water again. "As I thought," he said. "No better from this side. But nobody minds. Nobody cares. Pathetic, that's what it is."'

Who knows what Eeyore's early experiences had been, but certainly he lived now in a very Gloomy Place!

Depression from within

There is a sort of depression which seems to arise from inside and has no identifiable external cause. If only there were some particular reason for it, it might be easier to bear. It seems so stupid to have to confess that 'although I have a good husband, three lovely children, a nice home, no worries about money, yet I feel so depressed. How can anyone understand or sympathize with that? They will just tell me to count my blessings or pull myself together.'

Some people are liable to depressive mood swings because of their physical make-up. Other people have had deep wounds in childhood. Still others have patterns of living which lead to depression. Whatever the cause, those closest to them will need help and support in understanding.

Frozen rage

Some psychiatrists have regarded as axiomatic the fact that depression is the opposite of deep-seated rage or anger. This rage is by no means apparent to the casual observer, nor even to the depressed person himself. Depressed people often seem too lethargic to show much anger. Yet there may be a clearly noticeable tone of anger in the person's voice, and an outburst of anger sometimes relieves the depression for a time.

The stressful, explosive feelings which frustration generates are very similar to the sensations of anger. If they cannot be released outwardly, allowing the level of emotional tension to return to normal, they become 'bottled up' and turn back on themselves. These feelings do not simply evaporate. They must be dealt with, either externally by an outburst or some more reasoned expression, or else by being 'swallowed' inside where they go on smouldering. Either way is potentially dangerous.

Attempted suicide

Attempted suicide is usually a cry for help. This bottled-up rage expresses itself in a violent form – sometimes the only way it can come out. An overdose of drugs or slashing of wrists is a powerful demonstration of anger turned into *self* abuse. It has the desired effect of drawing attention to feelings which are not expressible adequately in any other way.

It also makes the onlookers feel very bad and guilty, which is an effective way of releasing angry feelings. If friends and relatives can understand this, it may help them to contribute more sensitively to the situation and not just react angrily in return.

The wisdom of the Bible applies directly to this situation in these words from Psalm 4: 'Be angry and do not sin: commune with your own heart on your bed.' In other words, recognize the situation honestly and then think quietly about its causes. Own up to your own faults in the situation; learn what areas of personal growth and self-control are needed; and think how a broken relationship can be restored to a greater degree of mutual understanding. The letter to the Ephesians adds further wise advice: 'Do not let the sun go down on your anger.'

Many of us find it very hard to handle strong feelings. We have never been able to trust anyone deeply enough to allow ourselves to be really truthful about either our love or our hate. So we live our lives at half pitch, afraid to be honest and expose ourselves to hurt. Our relationships feel safe only if they are superficially pleasant and sweet, and we go to endless lengths of self-deception to keep them that way.

We hide from ourselves and from others the strong feelings that make us uncomfortable. To keep them in check, we may go very quiet, or leave the room, or become depressed. Our inner negative feelings seem so powerful and provocative that we feel sure someone will hit back and destroy us if we express them. So we creep about, carrying our burden of nastiness, for fear of retribution.

De-pressed
It is this burden which presses down – or de-presses

us. It is the sort of feeling Brian would have experienced. His father seemed strong and big and powerful. It was not safe to take him on in combat. He may have tried, by rebelling in some way, but he soon learnt that a worse fate befell him. Or he may not even have tried to defend himself. He may simply have assumed it was pointless to try because defeat was a foregone conclusion.

But inside he would be thinking, 'You failed me: you are no good to me: I hate you: I wish you were dead.' Of course, it would be too dangerous to direct those strong bad feelings against his father. So instead they turn in against himself and he thinks, 'I am a failure: I am no good to anyone: I hate myself: I wish I could die.'

There are times when someone suffering from the frozen rage associated with 'endogenous' depression needs professional help, not only to expose the deep-rooted origins of injury but to obtain adequate help in the process of recovery and healing.

Chapter Three

Depression from Without

Although we are all so dependent on heredity and the factors which influence our early years, the circumstances of our adult life can also be a cause of depression. We all know that inability to pass an examination, failure to get promotion, continuous frustration in buying or selling a house, and a hundred-and-one other external events can precipitate a bout of gloom which seems to bring life almost to a standstill.

Depression is frequently triggered off by some identifiable crisis which leaves us with a sense of loss, change and emptiness. The most obvious of these is the pain of bereavement and the end of an important and loving relationship.

Arthur Smith used to go out for a little walk every day with his wife, but now she was no longer there. He sat alone; no point in going out; nowhere to go; too tired anyway. Most of his activity and thought had centred on Mary, but she had died three months ago. Now everything had changed. The sun had gone, and he just sat there. Too much effort to eat, and he didn't want to go down to the pub. He felt rather a wet blanket these days. Arthur was lonely, missing Mary very severely. He was going through the inevitable process of grief, and depression is often a part of that.

But there are many other 'bereavements' which we suffer – the loss of a limb in a car accident; the failure of one of our bodily functions because of an illness, or increasing age.

Our body is the means by which we communicate with the outside world and which reflects the way we feel about ourselves. Therefore, if our body becomes disfigured or spoilt in some way, that can have profound repercussions upon our inner feelings of self-esteem and identity.

Jane Blower had had a major operation. The recovery process had not gone straightforwardly; she now had recurrent distress and pain, and had to be very careful about her diet. There were often times when she was quite unable to work. And she never knew when one of these attacks would come. Holidays, parties, and even ordinary routine events had become uncertain. She could no longer trust her body to behave itself and her whole life became tentative.

Normally she was brave and cheerful but from time to time, after one of these attacks, she would sink into tearful gloom, saying that she was useless, unreliable and a failure. She was completely restricted and frustrated by this body which would not let her do the things she wanted to do and which other people were doing.

Life brings other losses such as retirement, redundancy, change of house, or the loss of possessions in a fire, and all these things can produce a profound sense of emotional discomfort and dislocation. Depression produced by some specific stress situation in our external circumstances is called 'reactive depression'.

Christians are human too!

Everyone is exposed to the unpredictable results of human relationships and the events of life. Christian people who believe in God and have some experience of his faithfulness in their lives are not exempt from depression. Many great saints of old, as well as many little-known people, know how strange and distressing it is to find that their previous joy in God has vanished.

They share the experience of David, in Psalm 13: 'How much longer will you forget me, Lord? For ever? How much longer will you hide yourself from me? How long must I endure trouble? How long will sorrow fill my heart day and night?'

The fact that a person is a Christian does not mean he ceases to be a normal human being!

Chapter Four

Recognizing the Symptoms

What does depression feel like? How can we recognize it in ourselves and others?

People react to depression in different ways. Not everyone will have all the symptoms. Depression itself varies in intensity, so the more serious it is the more symptoms there will be. Many people go through phases of vague and generalized unhappiness. Fewer suffer to the extent of having to be admitted to hospital. Indeed, it quite often happens that the symptoms are hardly recognized. I have a friend who is aware of her inner depression only when she finds herself constantly sighing.

It takes people in different ways. Some go on an overspending spree. Others start an eating binge, or embark on almost compulsive promiscuous sexual adventures. All these are evidence of underlying emotional turmoil. They are often forms of behaviour which are really designed to relieve depression in some way.

Admitting the truth

People sometimes feel quite annoyed when they are told that they are depressed. The word depression seems to carry with it overtones of failure and inadequacy. They deny feeling depressed. They are just tired, or not sleeping well, or they have lost their appetite. But depressed? 'Oh no, I'm not depressed.'

Our culture has not encouraged people to come to terms with their emotions or express them – to themselves, or to others. The show must go on, regardless! A heart attack, gastronomic or other disorders are allowed, but not emotional troubles. It is because we are not able to handle emotional pain that some of us are gradually overtaken by chronic depression, which often comes to the surface only in the form of a physical illness.

The case of the teacher

Jean Williams was a teacher, competent, efficient, hardworking and conscientious. She picked up a throat infection and her doctor gave her a few days off work. To her surprise she found that when the time came to return to work she just could not face it. The thought of having to make decisions and take responsibility made her curl up. She had found it increasingly hard to keep going during the previous months and was appallingly tired. It had been such an awful effort to get out of bed. She had been getting more and more irritable, but making a great effort to control herself. Suddenly everything caught up with her.

But she could not admit to herself that she was depressed. And she certainly did not want her colleagues to see that word written on her medical certificate. She felt positively guilty, as if she were just malingering. When she did at last accept the fact that she was emotionally ill, it was a great relief.

Visits to a psychotherapist helped her discover that her present distress was linked with unresolved feelings in childhood. Her father had died tragically, and because her mother had collapsed with grief, Jean had felt that she ought to 'mother' the other children and keep the family going as best she could. All this caring, first for her brothers and sisters, and then for the deprived children at school, proved too much. Her body gradually forced her into a situation in which she had to look at her own underlying need to be dependent and cared for.

When she was a child, the painful feelings had been pushed underground. But they had been carried along into adult life, erupting from time to time. Jean had tried to ignore these eruptions, which usually took the form of a minor physical ailment. However, there came a time when she could no longer ignore the intense emotional pain she was feeling. The process of healing involved re-experiencing the emotions of fear, anger and rejection which she had felt as a young child.

It often takes courage to recognize and admit that we are depressed. But that admission is the first essential step towards a greater freedom and enjoyment of life.

So tired!

From the outside, depression looks passive and negative, but inside much activity is going on. We may not be aware of it but a great turmoil is taking place which absorbs a lot of emotional energy. It is not surprising, then, that sheer weariness – to a greater or lesser degree – is one of the commonest features of depression. Both body and mind seem to slow down, because so much energy is taken up by the emotions.

It is difficult to remember things and concentrate. Even the most trivial decisions become almost impossible. We can't decide whether to go by car or train, or better still, not go at all.

The business man begins to look for ways of disguising these reactions but before long his colleagues start to comment on his increasing 'remoteness' and lack of involvement.

The housewife may begin to feel panic-stricken when, having made the physical effort of getting to the shops, she cannot remember what to buy. The mounting pile of ironing, which she cannot begin to tackle, threatens to upset her fragile emotional balance. Everything becomes too much. It seems impossible to do anything about it. Even sewing on a button feels like climbing Everest.

All this lethargy can increase the sense of guilt which may already exist. How can we be so feeble? Other people cope. It can be a tremendous relief to be reassured that this is all part of the over-all condition. It is not another proof of our total uselessness.

Out in the cold

There is also a general disengagement from what is going on around us: a lack of response. Things which formerly gave pleasure now leave us cold. Shakespeare's Hamlet is a classic case. He had a dark sense of foreboding about the disasters which were overtaking the kingdom. He was completely down-hearted.

'... I have of late lost ... all my mirth,' he says. He goes on to describe the beautiful world, sky and sunsets which he enjoyed before. Now they seem '... a foul and pestilential congregation of vapours'! He looks at his friends, whom he knows to be noble, gifted, intelligent, and he says: '... and yet to me, what is this quintessence of dust? Man delights me not: no, nor woman neither.'

Those may not be the words we would use – but we recognize the feeling. Depression produces a loss of response which invades our inner world and robs it of meaning. Everything seems black: there is no light at the end of the tunnel.

Fears and tears

No wonder that many people are desperately afraid they are going out of their mind. They are sufficiently in touch with reality to know that their reactions are irrational. But at the same time they are quite unable to become 'themselves' again. They think they are the only one who has ever felt like this, that no one can understand what it is like. Of course each person has to suffer his own depression. But one of its most painful aspects is the thick fog which separates the depressed person from the many others who may understand all too well!

Tears well up quickly, especially if someone is kind and sympathetic. This can be embarrassing. No one likes to be so vulnerable. It seems to add personal humiliation to an already painful situation. There is also the thought of the other person's distress or embarrassment. On the whole, people prefer to do their crying (and when they are depressed they do plenty of it) in private. It's as if the tears flow from a deep, unhealed wound of sadness within.

This inner sadness also expresses itself in deep involuntary sighs. It's a kind of physical attempt to shift the weight of an inner burden. At the depths of depression, people cannot even gain release through tears – they just cannot respond to anything emotionally any more.

Sleep disturbed

Night-time brings little relief. Sleep comes, but so does wakefulness, and there is a regular *disturbance of the sleep pattern*. In the early hours we may wake up and lie awake for a long time, perhaps only managing to fall asleep again just before it is time to get up. Everything seems worse in the night. We are an easy prey to the torment of all those joyless thoughts and fears.

When we relax in sleep our conscious mind 'goes off duty'. The unresolved material which lies buried below the level of consciousness begins to surface. It wears a disguise, which is why the coded language of our dreams is so difficult to understand. If the feelings associated with our dream material become too frightening and threaten to overpower our emotions, the sentries of our conscious mind rush to the rescue and we wake up at once. We may not be able to recall the dream (many people say they never dream). However, most people can recall the intense feeling of relief when they wake up and discover that something was only a dream. The disconcerting effects of this often last into the day, until the messages from below have been pushed back into unconsciousness again.

When someone is acutely depressed, the inner conflict surfaces more easily. The daytime guards try to do their duty but it is harder to keep the turmoil at bay. In their absence at night, the buried resentments, fears and terrors make their unwelcome presence felt all too painfully. The sentries, once recalled, cannot go off duty again, so there is no likelihood of unguarded sleep for several hours.

Prolonged sleeplessness in emotional discomfort is intolerable. Most people resort to sleeping-pills which take over and block out this nocturnal activity. It is a sensible and necessary expedient, but it does not solve the underlying problem.

The morning after

Having survived the rigours of the night, day dawns and spreads out like a yawning chasm to be got through somehow – though there seems little point. A sleepless night just adds to the general lack of enthusiasm. Often the misery of depression seems worse in the morning. There is no incentive to get up, and in fact bed seems to offer some sort of protection from life's demands. By the end of the day they may seem more manageable.

Depression removes our sense of proportion: perception becomes distorted. If I have a disagreement with my husband, I am sure he does not love me any more and the whole marriage was a ghastly mistake. If one of my colleagues at work walks past without a smile, I am sure I'm unpopular with the whole office staff and no good at my job. Everything is made worse by the feeling that life will always be like this. Hope disappears. Joy is something for other people.

We seem to ache all over inside, almost as though there is a physical injury. The experience is similar to physical ill health. We know it is not normal and healthy but we cannot consciously control it. This inner ache fills our thoughts. We become inward-looking. Why bother to talk to the hairdresser about summer holidays or fashions, when they seem to be totally irrelevant?

Food

Another clue to depression is our attitude to food. All food may become uninteresting or tasteless: there is not much enjoyment in preparing or eating it. Without even trying, we lose a few pounds in weight. On the other hand, food may represent some sort of consolation. Bars of chocolate, biscuits, sweet cakes (anything which does the figure no good!) become particularly comforting. It is not because we are hungry: usually we are not. We are simply trying to relieve the inner emotional hunger.

Food has always been more than a means of survival. It is a basic symbol of loving care and nourishment. In the earliest months of life a mother tells her baby she loves him by the way in which she feeds him. The baby does not understand the words, but he is well aware of the quality of love in the experience of feeding.

Sharing a meal has been an age-long gesture of

friendship and love between friends. It is no accident that Christians remember the death of Jesus Christ – God's most eloquent message of love to mankind – in a shared meal: the 'communion'.

When the spirit within us is heavy, messages and symbols of love are hard to appreciate. We may turn away from food in the same way as we turn away from gestures of love from a friend. Or when the spirit feels starved and hungry, we are apt to gobble up anything which may hold some promise of satisfaction. For some, alcohol produces a temporary sense of well-being. But, as with drugs, the effect wears off and another intake is required. Indeed, it is likely that alcohol leads to an even greater sense of depression, like 'hope deferred'.

Sexual drive

Another clue to recognizing depression is a *diminished sexual drive*. There is no pleasure in 'the chase' and no interest or energy for sexual activity. This sometimes complicates a marriage relationship. Silence or lack of response by a depressed partner (specially if the depression is not recognized) can easily be misinterpreted as a withdrawal of love.

The unconfident husband may quickly become anxious about his adequacy as a husband and lover. The wife may become suspicious and afraid that her husband's attentions are directed to some other woman, and that she is not attractive enough. Both these attitudes may be groundless – though they may produce reactions which really endanger the relationship.

Physical symptoms

Some people become anxious and frightened when they are depressed. They may develop all sorts of physical anxiety symptoms such as sweating, trembling, heart-thumping, dizziness or stomach troubles. These are uncomfortable side-effects but will settle down when the depression lifts.

Self-doubt

Although not everyone has these symptoms all the time, any one of them can lead to a *loss of self-confidence*. Whatever behaviour may result from a depressed spirit, there is an underlying feeling: 'I am inadequate, a failure, no good.' The conviction goes so deep that no amount of reassurance from loving friends has much impact. Even though the depressed person knows in his mind that he is not in fact so useless, he cannot convince himself of it.

When time stands still

A curious change in our perception of the passage of time often occurs. In normal life the hours speed by and our internal clock can virtually function by itself. But depression seems to make time almost stand still. The watch says eleven o'clock. After what seems like an hour, the hands still register only an incredible five past eleven. We have to make a conscious effort to calculate whether it is Tuesday or Friday.

It is easier to recognize the significance of all these changes when depression is acute, particularly if it is related to some recognizable cause. It is more difficult when depression has become a settled pattern of life, so that it seems part of our personality:

'Oh, I'm just fundamentally lazy,' or 'I'm a born pessimist.'

Nervous breakdown

In T. S. Eliot's *The Cocktail Party*, Edward Chamberlayne explains to his psychiatrist that he is on the edge of a nervous breakdown.

'Nervous breakdown is a term I never use,' replies Sir Henry Harcourt Reilly. 'It can mean almost anything.'

It is like the term 'headache', merely a description of what it feels like, not a statement of what is happening.

There are various reasons why our emotions seize up. One of them is an overwhelming depression which overtakes us and prevents us from functioning normally. We are out of action temporarily, for one reason or another, and so can rightly be said to have broken down. Powerful emotions have been accumulating behind the dam and have broken through, causing an incapacitating flood.

Our discerning psyche knows when open and straightforward expression of our ills would be too much for us, or others, to cope with and it lets them out in an oblique form which calls attention to our plight. The purpose of healing is not simply to gather them up and put them back where they were, but to assess the causes, the needs, the potential – and probably carry out major reconstruction so that the emotional energy can be harnessed and become powerful to a constructive purpose. Healing, in this situation, needs professional help from a psychiatrist or psychotherapist.

Chapter Five

Danger Points
and People at Risk

The idea that childhood constitutes the happiest days of our life is a myth! The present moment for a child is intense with delight and pain. Joys, fears, anxieties carry with them the thought that it is always going to be like this. There is only a little life experience to balance this impression. Unhappy children are additionally vulnerable because they do not know the words in which to express their misery, and so gain the support or comfort they need. Usually they lack the skill to know the precise cause of the trouble. They only know that they are unhappy.

Simon

One little boy, Simon Field, was admitted to hospital for observation. He was a pale, thin seven-year-old, quiet and withdrawn, seeming to take little interest in what was happening, except that he cried piteously when his mother had to leave him. His mother was very worried, as she watched him gradually change from a wiry bright-eyed mischief to an irritable, tired, dispirited child who played with food instead of eating it, and who cried when she made him go to school. The doctor had assured her there was nothing wrong with him, but obviously all was not well. His school teachers also remarked on the fact that he was not doing well these days.

Six months previously his father had left home and gone to live with a woman who had three children of her own. Mr Field was careful to keep regular weekly contact with Simon. They went fishing together as before, but this time with the other children too. They had good times in the new home, but Simon felt he did not know the new lady and could not get used to hearing these other boys referring to his father as 'Dad'.

Saturdays seemed far apart and he felt deeply hurt that *he* had to leave his Daddy at bedtime, while the other three stayed. Why didn't Daddy love him any more? What had he done to make life go like this? Big questions preoccupied him constantly and he could not begin to find an answer. He sensed that his mother did not want to tell him, or talk about why she now spent so much time at work instead of being at home with him. Gradually his body began to speak for him, as he drooped and faded, until someone's attention was drawn to the degree of his inner pain.

How could Simon be helped? The answer he needed was for Daddy to come home and gradually to re-establish the sense of trust which had been broken. Could Mr Field do that and risk hurting the new family to some extent? Could Mrs Field be helped with her own feelings of outrage, guilt and loneliness, so that she could become more emotionally available to Simon – and even to her husband? Or had the situation become irretrievable?

Julia

On the other hand there was Julia Collins. She was eleven when her parents separated; an event which she hailed with profound relief. The explosive threats, angry silences, tears and endless arguments had gone on for too long. The comparative calm which now reigned was a welcome change. But she resolved that when she grew up she would never live like that. She would never allow herself to become vulnerable to any man.

As the years went by, she developed into a physically attractive girl with a good figure, so she had no difficulty in acquiring boyfriends and she had great fun with them, but inside she was hard, ungiving and cynical. Little wonder that Julia's own marriage followed her parents' into the divorce court, and her own daughter was left to make what she could of it.

Without doubt, children suffer great damage when their love relationships are broken. They often suffer more than the adults in the long run. Marriage breakdown is a *very* serious matter.

Growing up

Children frequently express their feelings through their behaviour: it is easier than formulating words. Sickness, delinquency, truancy can all be ways of expressing an inner depression of spirit, boredom and aimlessness.

Adolescence is a turbulent time too. It is the time

for trying to establish our own personal identity, breaking loose from parental values, and questioning everything. We swing from splendid independence to halting dependence and uncertainty, and a desperate need for someone to hold on to.

As the adolescent struggles to achieve emotional separation from his parents and background, he often goes through the pain of depression and loss. Below the surface he is uncertain and doubtful about himself. He is acutely aware of his own inadequacies. At this time, too, he is often under considerable pressure from his school and his parents to produce good results in important exams.

The accumulation of internal and external pressure may become too great and he may collapse into complete inability to do anything. It is distressing for parents to see the emotional paralysis which takes over.

Some adolescents become entangled in an emotional alliance with possessive parents who cannot let their children go and explore life on their own. Both protest their wish for freedom, but unseen chains hold them together in a bondage of frustration, which sometimes shows itself in depression and frozen rage.

It is important that adolescents find work (their road towards independence) and that it is work in which they can express themselves creatively. Much boredom, vandalism and delinquency in our present society is an angry and depressed protest about the way young people feel themselves to be devalued, at a time when their own inner esteem is at a precarious level. And present unemployment levels, making it difficult for school leavers to find any work, let alone suitable jobs, can only add to the problem.

It is hard to know how to help, but some creative outlet must surely be found. The trouble is that money is also a vehicle for adolescent independence and so work and money become linked. Unpaid work may therefore be only a partial answer.

Loneliness

Loneliness and too much isolation is a very common gateway to depression. This miserable emptiness is heavily reinforced in people who are longing for companionship or marriage. It has a vicious circle quality about it. If only they could move out of the feeling of helpless need, they might be more likely to find a mate. But they feel they cannot move out until they have found someone.

This sometimes applies to other situations where desperate longings remain unfulfilled – young women remain childless, or some part of life remains closed.

Many people have found that eventually relief and joy have come. They have been able to accept and co-operate with the fact that some much-desired element in life is unattainable. Christian people know that their longings are all known to their heavenly Father, and that he will open up new areas of personal fulfilment if they are prepared for the hard task of letting go the hankerings. The Bible assures us that God has a purpose for the life of each individual. If we *can* reach the hard point of relinquishing those precious hankerings and trust the wisdom of God, in faith, we find that we grow into a much richer experience of life. Not easy!

As the years go by, the regrets and frustrations build up if they are not dealt with and discharged. Middle age, with its adjustments to change and incipient reminders of mortality, can create its own depression. Loss of youthful powers, decline in sexual function, and family changes all bring their stress and need for reassessment.

Old age

Old age brings its own special serenity, but also its losses, fears and loneliness. They can be very real, painful and depressing, especially if they have not been prepared for well in advance. As we grow older, we rely increasingly on our inner, and not our outer, resources.

Our bodies feel less energetic. We withdraw from involvement (though not from interest) in the outside world. We become more concerned with our memories and thoughts. The quality of our personal relationships, our spirituality and our own creativeness in younger years will frequently determine the way in which we face and handle the changes and the sadness which old age can bring to our body and to our mind.

I have a clear memory of a certain man I used to know – white-haired, with a calm, gentle face. He was no longer the strong leader he had been in former years. He was experiencing the loneliness caused by the death, one by one, of his contemporaries. And at his age they would not be replaced by other friends. He could not get about very easily. He used to listen wisely to the exploits of his younger friends. He had known deep sorrow and joy, and most of the things that life can bring to a man.

He also knew God. It was obvious that in the long inactive hours he held two-way communication with God and that the potential loneliness and uncertainty of life was transformed for him into calm, trustful faith based on years of experience of a faithful God. That sort of old age is so attractive!

On the other hand, we all know old people who are querulous and troublesome. They do not seem to have learnt anything from life except how to be demanding. They seem bitter and neglected, and it is hardly surprising that they feel unloved and lonely. Their depression is easily visible below the surface.

Are we at risk?

From all this it is possible to build up some kind of picture of people who are more likely than others to succumb to depression. They will be those who feel basically dependent on others and unsure of themselves; are very sensitive to rejection and disapproval; who find it difficult to say 'no' and set limits for themselves; are anxious about other people's opinion of them, and need to be liked and respected. They are perfectionists, ambitious and energetic.

They are particularly vulnerable to loss and have often suffered the loss of someone significant in childhood. They are often inflexible and feel a need to control their environment as a way of minimizing uncertainties and insecurities. They often find it difficult to delegate and thus be at someone else's mercy. They also find it difficult to handle aggression and hostility, because they are afraid of losing the love they need, or of losing control of their own rigidly clamped anger.

It may not be a cheering thought, but most of us come into one or other category!

It is no good saying, 'Oh, I'm like that: it's the way I was made.' Our responsibility is to change and grow out of unsatisfactory behaviour patterns which we have evolved. We begin to do this by noticing when we feel tense or threatened, or when good friends point out some awkwardness. We have to talk to ourselves and unearth our hidden fears and motives so that we can wrestle with them. We are never too old to change, if we will be humble enough to admit the need!

Chapter Six

What can be Done?

Sooner or later, if the depression is obvious, someone will ask whether we have been to the doctor. We often feel reluctant to go, because we do not quite know what to expect, or how bad he will think our condition is. It is always sensible to ask for help even if we do feel rather foolish. It is a sign of health to acknowledge need and a sign of an unhealthy attitude to ignore it.

The doctor will probably ask us how we feel, how the symptoms show, how long we have been like this, how we spend our working time and free time. He will enquire into eating and sleeping patterns and generally try to get the feel of what life is like for us.

He will then decide what is the most appropriate form of help. He may prescribe drugs, or a holiday, or whatever form of relief seems appropriate. He may think it is wise to refer us for a psychiatric opinion if the depression seems to be very acute and severe.

Many people resist this idea. They do not want to be thought 'mad': but that is a misunderstanding. A psychiatrist is simply a specialist in emotional disorders. Every hospital consultant is a specialist in something. It is old-fashioned prejudice which makes people think that emotional illnesses are in a different category from physical ones. They can be just as painful and disabling.

The psychiatrist may refer us back to the general practitioner, with advice about the best way to handle the situation. Or he may recommend admission to hospital for observation or treatment by drugs or ECT (electro convulsive therapy), or psychotherapy.

Antidepressant drugs

Antidepressants are the most common form of medication. There is an array of trade names which baffles the layman. The purpose of them all is to lift the heavy mood.

Prior to 1957 there was only one set of drugs. They are not now in widespread use, because they tend to be addictive. Nowadays tricyclic anti-depressants are usually prescribed – imipramine, amitriptyline, etc. Their purpose is to stimulate some of the brain mechanisms and to tranquillize others.

Doctors can experiment with a variety of these drugs to discover which is best suited to the patient's needs. Some produce too drowsy a state for comfort. Another group of antidepressant drugs – like Mianserin – have fewer side-effects but are sometimes less effective. A fourth group of antidepressant drugs called M.A.O.I.s are strong and more difficult to manage, in that they require strict dietary control. Cheese, chocolate, marmite and some other foods are forbidden. However, in spite of the drawbacks they are more effective for some people. It is very important that anyone using, or stopping the use of, antidepressant drugs should do so under the guidance of a medical practitioner.

ECT

ECT (electro convulsive therapy) under general anaesthetic is sometimes prescribed for patients who are in severe depressive states. This involves the controlled passage of an electric current through the brain. This treatment is administered two or three times a week until improvement begins to show. The number of doses can be from six to twelve according to the needs of the patient. This treatment is sometimes followed by difficulty in remembering things, but that passes off after a few hours. It has the advantage of working quickly and reliably to relieve profound states of depression and is sometimes tried in less severe cases when other treatments have failed. (It has been in use for over forty years, and no lasting harmful side-effects have been found.)

Psychotherapy

There is a whole spectrum of help available through talking about the problem, ranging from advice-giving to psychoanalysis. Carl Jung said that good advice is often a doubtful remedy, but it is generally not dangerous since it has so little effect! Its main value (in this context) is that it makes the advice-giver feel better.

Counselling is usually a discussion about the problem which involves thoughtful reflection, aided by questioning. The aim is the resolution of the immediate difficulty because of increased understanding.

Psychotherapy. The difference between skilled counselling and psychotherapy is hard to define. In psychotherapy feelings and emotions are uncovered of which the 'patient' has not been aware before. Unfinished business from the past which is being unconsciously and troublesomely swept along into the present can be resolved within the relationship between the therapist and the patient. The treatment may continue for some months on a regular basis.

Psychoanalysis is a further point along the spectrum. This is a long, demanding and expensive commitment (usually an hour every day for four years or more). It centres mainly on the patient's unconscious life, dealing largely with his dreams.

The aim of these last two methods is to achieve a basic change in behaviour and personality.

What does Chrisianity offer?

Christianity will not change our body chemistry, or our housing situation, or bring back a lost loved one. But Jesus Christ is able to change our *attitudes* to all these external things, as well as our attitude to relationships and to ourselves, which is often the basic root of the problem.

We can confess to him our needs or ordinary human weakness and fear, our hidden jealousies and anger, our readiness to push the blame on to other people, or our deliberate wrong-doings. He can make us aware of attitudes we had not realised, if we honestly want to know. He also has the authority to forgive us and make the slate clean by his death for our sins on the cross. He offers everyone who will come to him a new life which death itself cannot extinguish. And he has proved the reality of this by his resurrection. He has made it possible for us to have a personal relationship with God.

Dean Milner-White's prayer encapsulates the spirit of this relationship ...

'O Lord, when I awake and the day begins,
waken me to Thy presence:
waken me to Thine in-dwelling;
waken me to inward sight of Thee,
    and speech with Thee,
    and strength from Thee:
that all my earthly walk may waken into song
and my spirit leap up to Thee all day, all ways.'

That does not mean that we at once become totally free of all our wrong attitudes. But it does mean that as we draw constantly upon the resources of God – in prayer, in reading his Word to us (the Bible) and in worship, we can be changed. With God's help we can do battle with the influences within ourselves which constitute a down-drag. Sometimes the battle is long and hard, but the forgiveness of God and the power of God's Holy Spirit are always available for those who are genuinely intent on change and growth.

Added to this, there is the support of other Christian people, fellow-travellers on the road. We can share friendship with them: we can support one another when the going is hard: we can spur one another on in faith and understanding.

Psychotherapy can help us to become more aware of our own needs. The Christian faith does not dispense with the value of other forms of treatment, be they physical or psychological.

Successful treatment

When we are thinking about depression we have to consider the whole person – his inherited temperament, his childhood background, his present social circumstances, his physiological state and the balance of interaction within his network of relationships. None of these factors can be considered in isolation from the others.

The successful and lasting treatment of depression involves openly acknowledging its existence. If it is denied or suppressed in some way, it will become a recurring experience, or it will convert itself into some other disorder of the body, emotion or behaviour. Successful treatment includes resolving the conflicts that produce the depression – conflicts from within our inner life, or from outer circumstances. Then it is likely that when we recover we will not slip back again into that same pit.

Excessive dependence is an evidence of immaturity. It leaves us vulnerable to many things, including depression. Growth in trust and confidence is essential to healthful maturity. But we cannot achieve it in isolation. It requires understanding and co-operation from key family members. There is opportunity for growth in the three areas: our attitude to ourselves; the way we relate to other people; and the way we cope with, or modify, difficult environmental conditions.

Depression, by its very nature, is associated with separation, loss and change. Life itself is about endings, change – and new beginnings.

Almost everyone can expect to experience some degree of depression at some time in their life. Even Christians who have a personal faith in God who is the source of all joy and peace are not exempt. They may in fact suffer more than people who have no particular belief, because the depression brings with it a false sense of guilt. They think they are letting the side down; not being a good advertisement for what Christianity is all about. They do not understand that depression, like the common cold, is no respecter of persons.

The key

Sometimes people think Christians ought not to be depressed. This is a complete misunderstanding. Christians are human beings, sometimes depressed, sometimes ill, sometimes unemployed – subject to their inner feelings and outer circumstances, like anyone else.

'Christian', in *The Pilgrim's Progress* knew all about this when he was captured by Giant Despair and thrown into the 'nasty, stinking dungeon' in Doubting Castle. He and his friend Hopeful lay hungry, frightened and in distress for five days, constantly expecting the Giant to come and beat them again. They were at their wits end, until Christian suddenly remembered that he possessed a key called 'Promise'. When he turned this key in the lock of the dreadful prison, the doors flew open and Christian and Hopeful ran out to safety.

I wonder which promise he used! God has given us so many in the Bible. It might have been:

'I will *never* leave you nor forsake you' (Hebrews 13:5)

or, 'Resist the devil and he *will* flee from you' (James 4:7)

or, '... neither life nor death ... nor anything else in all creation will be able to separate us from the love of God which is in Christ Jesus our Lord' (Romans 8:39).

We would like to ask for instant healing from this painful and distressing condition, but often healing comes slowly. If we were relieved of the pain instantaneously we would be very tempted to go rushing on with life and not stop to ask what caused it all and what changes need to be made. Although instant relief may be more comfortable, it may deny us a real chance to understand ourselves, to grow, and to increase in faith and maturity.

Religious doubts

In addition to the other symptoms, Christians suffering from depression will be prey to religious doubts. They feel that God has abandoned them. Their prayers seem to hit the ceiling. The Bible becomes meaningless and its rich promises look like a mockery. Just when they need help and comfort to ease the desolation, there is none to be found, and they begin to doubt their own sincerity and wonder whether Christianity was ever a reality.

All this is compounded if well-meaning friends

add to their own sense of guilt by urging them to search their souls for some hidden sin, which surely must have caused this misery. Job, in the Bible, had friends like that, and 'miserable comforters' they were!

Deadened reactions to everyone and everything are in the very nature of depression. The Christian's already battered emotions have no energy to reach out to God in prayer or Bible study, to receive stimulation from Christian fellowship, or even to appreciate God's continuing love. A thick fog prevents them from perceiving that God is still there. He has not gone away. He is quite able to hear their cries, but because they are partially blind and deaf emotionally they cannot take this in.

This sense of alienation can produce, for some people, the conviction that they have committed the 'unforgivable' sin. They do not really know what it is, but they feel they have overstepped the mark and gone beyond hope of restoration. This, again, is all part of the general impression of failure – of being abandoned by God and unable to find him again – which depression often brings.

But it was God who took the first step towards us. He loved us before we ever knew him. He is the Giver, the Lover: Christians are on the receiving end. We can do nothing to deserve or earn his goodwill. Love is a free gift. It has nothing to do with merit. So any feeling of being too bad for God is irrelevant.

God's love is not dependent on anyone's goodness or badness: it is dependent upon his own changeless commitment and faithfulness. Our *feelings* do not alter the truth of the statement. It may be an encouragement to point out that Job, Elijah and David all knew what depression was. And Paul, at times, felt utterly and unbearably crushed.

Holding on

Depression and its onset is usually like a sloping curve. It starts gradually and insidiously, but at the first stage this can be handled. Beyond a certain point it gathers strength and becomes unmanageable. The only thing to do then is to wait for it to pass over. Depression does not last for ever. Although it may take a long time, it does go. This makes it all the more important to recognize the symptoms.

The most effective way of dealing with incipient depression and its attendant doubts is to *remember* the faithfulness of God and deliberately recall his gracious and loving acts of goodness in our own experience. We need to hold on to the positives, so that when the negatives come we have something with which to balance them.

The New Testament book of Acts tells how Paul and Silas were flogged severely without any just cause and flung into a filthy jail. Yet at midnight they were singing songs! It wasn't out of high spirits, or because they were enjoying themselves.

They were singing as an antidote to depression, affirming God's faithfulness and their positive refusal to doubt, in spite of any temptation they might reasonably have had. This was a gesture of active trust – grasping the curve before it had a chance to take a nose-dive! It is vital that we make our gesture of active trust *at once*. If we hesitate it may be too late.

Chapter Seven

Living with
a Depressed Person

Mrs Baker was beginning to be quite worried. She sensed that her husband had changed. He seemed to have no enthusiasm for anything. She tried to discuss Robert's sudden progress at school and he answered in monosyllables. She wanted his opinion on certain repairs to the house and there was no response. She suggested a holiday and was met by the same dull lack of interest. Whatever subject she tried to talk about just fell flat. For weeks he had not shown her much affection and when she questioned him he just apologized and said half-heartedly that he would try to do better.

When she asked him outright what was wrong, he couldn't say: he didn't know: he wasn't ill but wasn't well. When she asked if she had done something to upset him he assured her she had not. But he still went on behaving as though he were totally bored with her. Mrs Baker was feeling bewildered, anxious and just a bit annoyed.

'I wish he would *tell* me what is the matter. Then I could *do* something about it. It's not *knowing* that is so awful. If there isn't anything wrong with him, why doesn't he pull himself together? It's all very well for him to sit there reading the paper or staring into space, but there are no end of things he could be doing to help me if only he would put his mind to it.'

It is very difficult living with someone who is depressed. At first we feel sympathetic. Then we begin to feel uneasy because in some way we feel responsible, but don't quite know what for. Have we caused it? Could we be doing something to help? But nothing we try seems to be any use. We try to be loving and comforting but that doesn't seem to ease the depression. So we leave him to his own devices – and he doesn't want that either! We feel vaguely guilty and somewhat irritated with this person who makes us feel so inadequate and useless.

That dreaded phrase 'pull yourself together' is usually an expression of our own frustration and annoyance. Not only may the lack of response make us feel helpless; the lethargy may throw an extra burden of work on us. In addition, depression is infectious! We may feel ourselves beginning to 'pick up the germs', and so we try to ward them off. Of course, it's totally useless to urge any depressed person to snap out of it and pull himself together. That is the very thing he cannot do. Being urged to do the impossible will only make him feel even more rejected and misunderstood. Even so, it is very hard to restrain our annoyance when we are suffering from someone else's depression!

How can I help?
It is also very sad to see the suffering of someone we love. 'What can I do? How can I help?' It may sound like cold comfort to be told that there is precious

little one can do except just *be there*, sensitively, without fuss. It is good to make the physical environment as pleasant as possible, with well-arranged flowers and appetisingly presented food. It is wise not to expect much appreciation.

This is a time when real love is called for: the sort described in 1 Corinthians 13, that is 'patient and kind, not arrogant or rude, not insisting on its own way, not irritable and resentful; bearing all things, hoping all things and enduring all things'.

Another tedious factor is the way people in depression seem to be obsessed with it. It is their major topic of conversation; they discuss it endlessly. They talk as though they are the only ones who really understand how terrible it is. Nothing else in life seems to have any meaning for them.

In the end we become extremely bored with the narrowness of their horizons. We have heard it all several times, and since no progress seems likely we really do not want to keep on going over the same ground. It is difficult not to leave them to get on with it. However, it is very important both emotionally and physically to try to stay with a depressed person. He needs the love and reassurance of his friends very specially at this time, although he is probably unable to respond. He does not want to be taken over, neither does he want to be alone.

Still down?

Depression hangs on with incredible persistence. People who have never experienced it find the time-lag hard to believe.

'Why are you still so down? Your mother has

been dead for three months now,' says someone to whom bereavement and depression are unknown.

'We had such a lovely day in the country yesterday, I thought you had recovered,' says another, who interprets the slightest lift in the cloud of depression as healing. Perhaps it is only those who have suffered themselves who can estimate the pain and the length of time it takes to pass.

A bewildered onlooker has often been heard to say, 'It is only a matter of will-power, really. If only she would make up her mind to master this thing she would soon get the better of it.'

No one enjoys being depressed. If it were so easily 'mastered' the solution would be simple. But depression is a matter of the emotions and the whole person, not simply of the will and the intellect. In the initial stages, the will can be called into play to some extent to resist downward drift, but beyond a certain point it is no longer possible.

The slowness and indecision of the depressed person, his tears, his preoccupation with himself and the feelings of futility that he engenders, all tend to produce impatience in the people who have to live with him. On a less conscious level, they may also pick up the hidden anger which may lie behind his depression. He may not realise that he is angry, but his attitudes, the tone of his voice and the choice of his words, give a clear message.

His family may give expression to the anger and hostility which he feels more easily than he can himself. They may be feeling relatively peaceful, but then he comes into the room, gloomy and taciturn, and before long everyone seems to be on edge and irritable, although nothing argumentative has been said.

If we respond with anger and rejection we reinforce the depressed person's feelings of helplessness and his conviction that he is unloved and misunderstood.

The situation is made more complex if the depression is unrecognized and the person tries to blame others for his unhappiness, or to deaden his conflicts with alcohol.

Gordon White had previously enjoyed his work as a salesman in a gents' outfitters. It was a small, but busy, branch of a chain store. Recently the manager had been making his life a misery for reasons he could not understand, and he was beginning to grow tired of constant petty criticism and unjust accusations. He knew he was doing his work properly – and was taking special care since the manager had become so prickly. In fact, he thought privately that the boss's work was sub-standard, not his own. One day the inevitable show-down came and he gave in his notice.

To his surprise, Mr Clark, the manager, admitted that he could not face the fact that he had lost his grip, and was afraid things were getting on top of him (though even then he did not recognize the symptoms as depression). Things then came out into the open, but Gordon could not help thinking what a great deal of annoyance and misunderstanding might have been avoided.

On the way up
Sometimes when people have been profoundly

depressed and have ground to a halt, they get outwardly worse before they get better. Distress and deep despair come to the surface and sometimes can lead to the desire to commit suicide. At times like these, particularly close support is necessary until they can see the world in its true perspective again and have lost their illogical burden of guilt.

When a depressed person is beginning to improve he may feel rather embarrassed that people have seen him when he was a tearful wreck. It is a sign of growing trust to believe that friends will not despise or criticise one's weakness.

He may also start to express his feelings more honestly. Other people may find some difficulty in handling his criticism and aggression. They may try to make him suppress these reactions again, or they may enter into open conflict. Sometimes they themselves become depressed. Depression never affects one person in isolation from his family and friends. Just as the two sides of a pair of scales affect each other, so the depressed person and his friends interact and counterbalance one another.

Mr and Mrs Weston had a problem. He was an executive with many business commitments which took him away from home, and often involved social occasions. He was intelligent, extrovert and go-getting. Mrs Weston was a charming person but she had terrible phases of real depression which immobilized her completely. She would weep end-lessly, feel an utter failure, and retreat to her bed for several days.

So acute was all this that eventually she sought

professional help and she gradually improved. The strange thing was that as she became more integrated and self-contained, her husband spent more and more time on the golf course. It seemed that in some way he felt threatened by his wife's increasing ability to hold her own. In some way he needed to have a 'weak' wife so that he could be 'strong'. When the balance changed he felt ill-at-ease and threatened by her in some vague way which he could not pin-point and did not care to think too much about. So he found his golf companions more comfortable.

If after the depression has passed the relationship between the depressed person and his family or friends simply returns to its former level of suppression or fractiousness, no real progress will have been made in spite of the painful experience. Progress means a greater degree of trust and openness, and the right sort of self-confidence.

Who should help?

The extent to which anyone should become involved in helping a severely depressed person depends on the nature and depth of the relationship. It is not appropriate for a casual friend to take on a major responsibility like this: this lies with closer relatives. It is better for casual friends just to be quietly available in a supportive way.

It is most important to remember that depression is a really painful experience. Sympathy does not necessarily help, but a sensitive understanding may ease the atmosphere.

Chapter Eight

Depression and Guilt

One characteristic of people likely to become depressed is the 'perfectionist' streak. They are over-conscientious and reliable. They work long hours, are meticulously honest and punctilious about detail, beyond all normal requirements. They have exceedingly high standards of personal behaviour.

Psychologists would describe this kind of person as having a powerful 'superego'. That is to say, he carries about within him an unrealistically harsh and merciless 'policeman' who never goes off duty and is always on the watch for the slightest misdemeanour. Consequently, any breach of the 'policeman's' inflexible standards of law and order is impossible. They must be kept rigidly.

Should there be a slip, the sense of failure and the fear of punishment is severe. The feeling of guilt always dogs these people's footsteps. Their inner superego is frowning in disapproval, creating great internal discomfort with its accusation, 'You've failed – again! You are no good!' An over-powerful superego is a very depressing companion.

People who are in the despair of a deep depression will inevitably have a distorted view of themselves. They will feel guilty and responsible for things with which they cannot remotely be associated – such as a car accident three hundred miles away. A gloomy perspective on life usually trails guilty feelings along with it. This is a temporary sense of guilt.

Some people experience swings of mood varying from excessive wellbeing to excessive gloom. This 'manic depression' seems to arise from a physiological cause and may have no direct link with the superego, in that the same person will have the opposite view of himself and his guilt at different stages of the mood swing. Unfortunately none of this is amenable to reason.

False guilt

The offence may be trivial – or no offence at all in real terms (forgetting to deliver a casual message, for instance), but the sense of guilt is painful, nonetheless. This is called 'false guilt' because it has no realistic basis. True guilt exists when some actual harm has been done to ourselves, to someone else, or to society. False guilt, engendered by an overbearing superego, may be the result of too strict an upbringing, or the feeling of dependence on people who are more powerful than we are. It is important for our sense of wellbeing to have their approval and support. So their standards must be kept and nothing must be done which might lose us their sympathy. The painful fear of losing goodwill on which we depend feels the same as the pain of guilt. False guilt is mainly about *fear* of broken relationships. True guilt is about the *fact* of someone having been harmed.

The person with the too-powerful superego feels he is responsible for everything. He also has the inbuilt assumption that he is likely to be wrong. So it's easy to manipulate him. For instance, if the office manager will readily take to himself all the blame for some inaccuracy, an unscrupulous colleague can manoeuvre him into taking on more work. It is difficult for him to stand his ground and handle conflict, because he's afraid of offending someone.

Conscience

Superego and conscience are not the same. Conscience is an objective sense of right and wrong, but it is not infallible. It is influenced by culture and custom. Superego is a subjective feeling which directs a person from within, regardless of external and absolute standards.

True guilt is constructive and healthy. It protects us from injurious behaviour. It promotes social harmony and personal peace of mind. Guilt is not linked with depression for everyone. But if true guilt is denied or not recognized, the person concerned may only begin to realize how much he is hurting himself when he becomes acutely depressed.

Keith Farmer was having problems. Nothing seemed to work out right for him. He kept putting off the jobs he had to do. He had constant rows with his wife. He was tired and depressed. His one bit of pleasure in life was the affair he was having with a woman they had met on holiday. He had silenced his initial qualms of conscience by telling himself that everyone does it – that he deserved a bit of fun.

Gradually he found himself doing other things that went against the grain of his strict church and school values. He was drinking slightly more than he could manage. He compromised at work with lies, and fiddled his expense account. He felt free of the inhibitions his religious background imposed on him. But it was a dangerous freedom. Previously his life had been fairly placid; now it seemed to have become a battle-ground. The fact that 'everyone does it' did not bring the assurance and confidence he wanted.

In his depression he realised he was faced with a choice. He could either carry on with his present way of life and continue to erode his self-esteem, or he could make a clean sweep and re-assess his basic values. He felt that the price he was paying for his present 'freedom' was too heavy, so he made a brave choice. He was amazed by the experience of emotional health and vitality which returned when he faced his guilt and dealt with it.

For many people, coping with depression means putting themselves back into touch with their feelings of true guilt, and then finding ways of resolving it.

Forgiveness

'Forgiveness' is a word which is significantly absent from psychological textbooks. It is, however, one of the key themes in the Bible.

'If we say that we have no sin', writes the apostle John, 'we deceive ourselves and there is no truth in us. But if we confess our sins to God (and therefore admit them to ourselves and to the person we have wronged) he will keep his promise and do what is right: he will forgive us our sins and purify us from all our wrongdoings.'

That is good news indeed, as Bunyan's 'Pilgrim' experienced when the crushing burden of guilt fell from his back at the cross of Jesus Christ, and he gave three leaps for joy.

In present-day society there is so much confusion that we are in danger of losing the salty and protective element of guilt. 'Anything goes' is a false standard. We are created with deeply engrained moral and emotional laws and values. Short-circuit them and things will inevitably go wrong. Sex-, abortion- divorce-on-demand may be a very convenient way to resolve our problems. But they often produce deeply destructive side-effects. Depression is perhaps the most common of these.

A society which has contradictory standards about moral values (war must be avoided at all costs; but brutal violence is constantly featured on television screens) leaves its people confused, with no clear sense of true and false guilt.

The fundamental need for stability in the early years of childhood was never understood as well as it is today. Yet the rate of divorce and the number of one-parent families was never higher. There is an urgent need in our day to regain a sense of personal responsibility and essential values. Vast numbers of people have lost a sense of true guilt, the protection that goes with it, and the health of forgiveness.

Chapter Nine

The Other Side
of the Valley

One of the few good things about depression is that, like all pain, it is saying something. If we can hear and understand the message, we may be able to make some necessary changes in our life-style or emotional economy. If we are to 'hear' the message we have to spend time, effort and honest consideration on ourselves and our situation. We may discover some recurring factor which always precipitates a depression, or some type of relationship which perpetuates our lack of self-confidence. We may need to discuss this with a wise and mature friend, or we may even require professional help in locating the cause and effecting the change.

Getting the message
Elinor Jarvis thought she was very happily married, until her husband took a job which involved a good deal of travelling. When he was away she was lost and lonely. When he came home she was full of energy and fun. She dreaded his absences.

'It's as if a part of me dies when he is not here. My life only means something when he is around.' She asked him frequently for reassurance of his love, and told him constantly that she could not live without him. She lived in constant fear that he might find another woman on one of his trips abroad, and leave her.

One day he did, sickened and weary of her clinging demands which held him in bondage. After a period of tempestuous letters, telephone calls and talk of suicide Elinor settled into a long period of depression. The cause was obvious. She had lost her husband.

She was bewildered and angry. She loved him so much and had tried so hard to please him. What had happened?

Elinor was born several years after her brothers and sister. She was always the 'baby', indulged by her parents and teased by her siblings. Her father was killed in a road accident when she was fifteen, but her capable mother kept the home together. Elinor did well at school, trained as a secretary. As an attractive twenty-one-year-old she married the promising young boss of her department. At thirty-one he walked out and her life was 'in ruins'. True, life as she had previously come to see and expect it, *was* in ruins. If Elinor could 'understand the message', however, she had the potential to build a fine house from the ruins.

Why?

What was the message behind the depression aroused by the loss of her husband? To find the message, she had to ask another question: Why had she lost him?

She had always been the 'baby' emotionally in

spite of her intelligence, her gaiety and apparent independence. She always needed people around her to boost her self-confidence and confirm her decisions. At first she had her competent mother in the background. Then she replaced her mother with a competent husband. She had told him many times, with alarming truth, 'I cannot live without you.'

In actual fact it is only a baby who cannot live without its mother. For the baby, its own needs are overpowering and urgent. They must be met. The absence of a mother seems to threaten the baby's existence.

The message for Elinor was that she had never grown up emotionally. She 'needed' her husband in a way which kept her permanently immature and which he eventually found manipulative, controlling and insatiable. She had felt that she was utterly dependent on his approval and goodwill. She never disagreed with him about anything important lest he should be displeased. She rarely used her own creative initiative and always tried to do what he would want.

Thus a part of her own essential personality was stunted and confined. She had never really made the opportunity, nor had the courage, to establish herself with her own identity. She was always afraid she might meet with some disapproval, and that she could not tolerate.

She put up with all sorts of inconsiderateness and inconvenience for the sake of keeping her husband always there. Eventually he was not there any more, because this became a boring and unproductive situation.

The slow miracle

What could she do about it? Elinor had to cope with a depression from two sides. Her husband's withdrawal involved the loss of a relationship which meant a great deal to her, and she was confronted with her own emotional immaturity which had contributed to the loss of her husband. That immaturity threatened every relationship into which she entered and was therefore quite a serious matter to her.

However, it was only this big crisis which made her begin to realise that this was her life-pattern of behaviour. It was an emotional system of helpless dependence upon which she had functioned for thirty-one years. Could she learn to rely on her own ability to meet her own needs without automatically running to someone else to make her complete?

If Elinor can do this how much more free and uninhibited her life will become: how much more attractive she will be as a person. But it will involve effort and take time. It may also involve some honest struggles with her family and friends as they adjust to support her changing and growing personality. She will then be able to offer what C. S. Lewis in his book *The Four Loves* describes as 'gift love', with no strings attached. Previously she was offering 'need love', which demands something in return.

If Elinor has a Christian faith she will also have the additional resource of prayer and strengthening faith in a faithful God as she grows into maturity.

Growth takes time: it is a slow miracle. It does not happen overnight!

Extreme dependency perpetuates a lack of self-confidence which can lead to chronic depression. Dependency has a way of feeding on itself and keeping the situation in stalemate. It is as addictive as drug-taking, and the withdrawal symptoms are equally unpleasant.

Dependence and helplessness are a position of power, in that they can control and manipulate other people. Elinor had, all unwittingly, been controlling her husband with her needs. (What about the old lady who dominates the whole household by her arthritis and runs the family without lifting a finger?) But a situation like that depends on other people going along with it. For good or bad reasons of their own, they are prepared to tolerate this dependence and encourage it: because it serves some need of their own.

Change is required from all parties if the stronghold is to be broken. This is what Elinor Jarvis' husband was doing when he walked out. Maybe that was the only way, if not the best, that he could handle the situation.

Sometimes post-natal depression carries with it some conflicting elements of dependence. The new mother is confronted by a totally helpless person who is utterly dependent on her. She must provide for this infant, although she has no reserves. She may have some lingering unresolved needs of her own to be dependent, though she will hardly be aware of them. This can set up a conflicting situation within her which shows itself as depression. (This sometimes happens in addition to the physically-triggered 'baby blues' which so many women experience.)

Change and acceptance

It is very difficult for any of us to see ourselves without someone to hold up a mirror for us. Certainly depression has an important message for us about the necessity of change. We may need to pay attention to our job, lifestyle, living accommodation or some other external circumstance which needs to be changed. It may be a message about the quality and nature of the relationships we make which are somehow less than fulfilling. Or we may need to change our attitude to some fact that we cannot alter.

The old prayer says:

'Grant me the serenity to accept the things I
    cannot change,
the courage to change the things I can,
and the wisdom to know the difference.'

We may have a good and wise friend with whom we can discuss these things. Sometimes people need some psychotherapeutic help if the knots are in a tangle.

The whole of the Christian gospel is about dealing with an inner sense of alienation or insecurity or fear, or the good old-fashioned word 'sin', which is responsible for a great deal of depression. The wonderful promise of God is that we can be forgiven if we genuinely repent, we can be restored to a relationship of love and trust with the living God, and we can be helped towards maturity.

We need no longer be a prey to helpless fears of disapproval, failure and need. We need not be anxious that we shall be separated from the sustaining and nourishing love-resources which we need.

A new life
Christians believe that spiritual life with God begins in this life – here and now. We can experience, increasingly, the calm of sins forgiven, of peace with God and assurance of heaven. One day, the limiting effects of this physical world and our mortality will be gone. We shall then continue our life with God in the fullest possible sense.

The picture-language of Isaiah expresses it beautifully:

'They will enter Zion with singing:
Everlasting joy will crown their heads:
Gladness and joy will overtake them,
And sorrow and sighing will flee away.'